1 Uppercase Letters Review

Writing A–Z

MW01196022

Have your child write their name and ...
workbook will help your child develop handwriting skills through fun and engaging activities. Review your child's progress as they complete each page.

■ Trace the letters A to Z.

A   B   C   D

E   F   G   H

I   J   K   L

M   N   O   P

Q   R   S   T

U   V   W   X

Y   Z

A B C D E F G H I J K L M N O P Q R S T U V W X Y Z

To parents/guardians: The first section of this workbook is designed to help your child review single letter formation. Practicing how to form individual letters will help your child write each letter neatly when they progress to writing full words.

■ Write the letters A to Z.

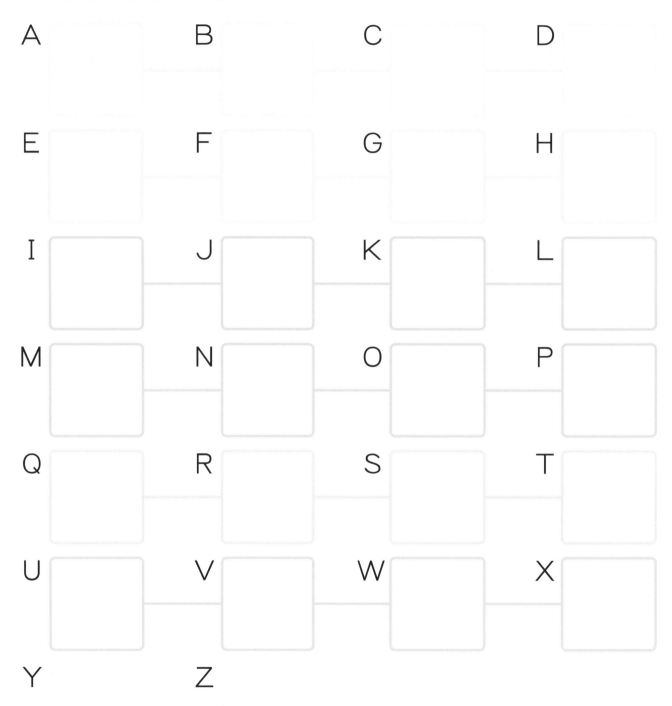

A   B   C   D

E   F   G   H

I   J   K   L

M   N   O   P

Q   R   S   T

U   V   W   X

Y   Z

A B C D E F G H I J K L M N O P Q R S T U V W X Y Z

Lowercase Letters Review

Writing a–z

Name

Date

/   /

■ Trace the letters a to z.

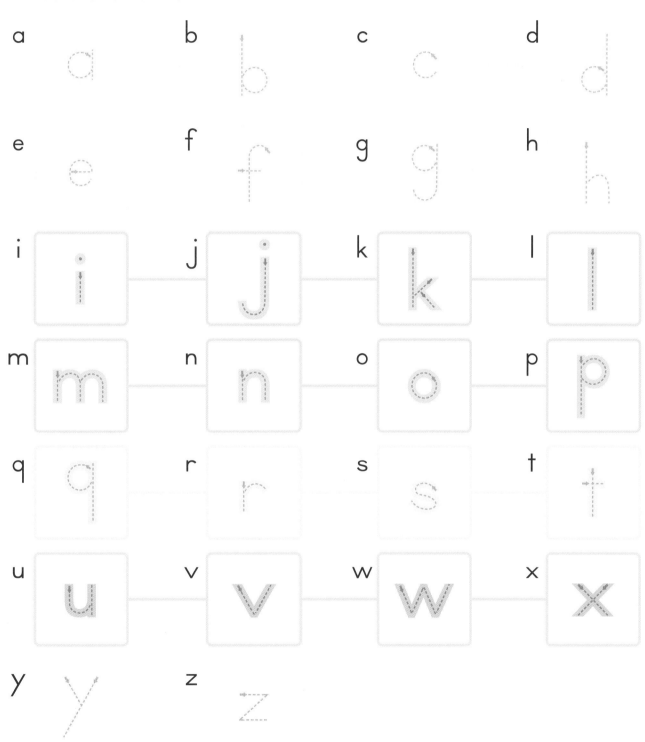

a b c d e f g h i j k l m n o p q r s t u v w x y z

■ Write the letters a to z.

a   b   c   d

e   f   g   h

i   j   k   l

m   n   o   p

q   r   s   t

u   v   w   x

y   z

a b c d e f g h i j k l m n o p q r s t u v w x y z

Ascending Letters
l, t, f, and h

Name

Date

/   /

To parents/guardians: In this activity, your child will practice writing ascending letters. These are letters that start in the top half of the sentence line.

■ Trace the letter. Then write the letter "l" in each word.

l

lion

ion   ion

shell

she   she

■ Trace the letter. Then write the letter "t" in each word.

t

tree

ree   ree

boat

boa   boa

To parents/guardians: If your child has difficulty writing any of the ascending letters, remind them to begin at the top red line and write with a downward stroke.

■ Trace the letter. Then write the letter "f" in each word.

f f f f f f f

frog

f r o g   r o g

leaf

l e a f   l e a

■ Trace the letter. Then write the letter "h" in each word.

h h h h h h h

hand

h a n d   a n d

lunch

l u n c h   l u n c

Ascending Letters
k, d, and b

Name

Date

/ /

To parents/guardians: Throughout this workbook, your child will practice forming letters and words neatly using sentence lines for guidance. Each sentence line is made up of four guidelines meant to help your child form letters legibly.

■ Trace the letter. Then write the letter "k" in each word.

k   k   k   k   k   k   k

king

king   ing

kick

ick   ick

■ Trace the letter. Then write the letter "d" in each word.

d   d   d   d   d   d   d

dog

dog   og

bird

bird   bir

■ Trace the letter. Then write the letter "b" in each word.

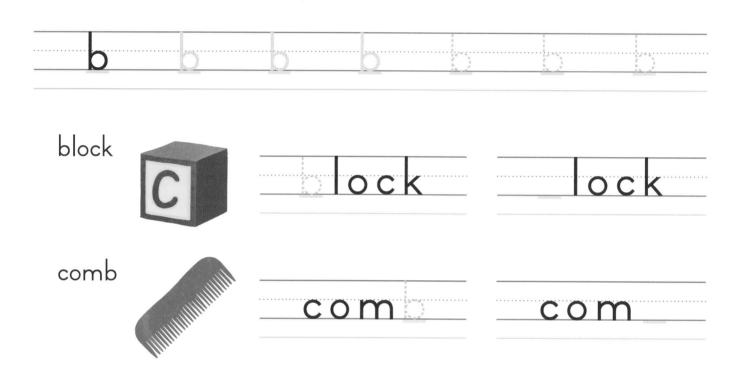

block

b l o c k   _ l o c k

comb

c o m b   c o m _

Ascending Letters Review

l, t, f, h, k, d, and b

Name

Date

/ /

To parents/guardians: On this page, your child will review how to neatly write all the ascending letters taught in this section. If your child can legibly write all the ascending letters, offer them a lot of praise.

■ Trace the letter. Then write the letter in each word.

lion

ion   ion   ion

tree

ree   ree   ree

frog

rog   rog   rog

hand

and   and   and

■ Trace the letter. Then write the letter in each word.

king

king   ing   ing

dog

dog   og   og

block

block   lock   lock

Descending Letters
j, y, and q

Name

Date

/   /

To parents/guardians: In this section, your child will practice writing descending letters. These are letters that drop below the bottom sentence line. It is important that your child writes letters that drop down to the bottom blue line.

■ Trace the letter. Then write the letter "j" in each word.

j   j   j   j   j   j   j

jewel

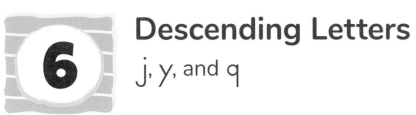

j ewel   ewel

jam

j am   am

■ Trace the letter. Then write the letter "y" in each word.

y   y   y   y   y   y   y

yarn

y arn   arn

day

da y   da

■ Trace the letter. Then write the letter "q" in each word.

queen

quilt

queen   ueen

quilt   uilt

Descending Letters
g and p

Name

Date
/ /

To parents/guardians: If your child only draws a short tail for a descending letter, remind them to draw the tail down to the blue line. Offer a lot of praise when your child writes the letter neatly and correctly.

■ Trace the letter. Then write the letter "g" in each word.

g   g   g   g   g   g   g

green

green   reen

flag

fla g   fla

■ Trace the letter. Then write the letter "p" in each word.

p   p   p   p   p   p   p

piano

piano   iano

soap

soa p   soa

Descending Letters Review

j, y, q, g, and p

■ Trace the letter. Then write the letter in each word.

jewel

jewel ewel ewel

day

day da da

queen

queen ueen ueen

flag

flag fla fla

soap

soap soa soa

Lowercase Letters

i, v, w, and r

Name

Date

/   /

To parents/guardians: In this section, your child will practice writing lowercase letters that are not ascending or descending letters. These letters should be written beneath the dotted middle line. If your child is unsure where to begin a letter, offer help by pointing to the dotted middle line.

■ Trace the letter. Then write the letter "i" in each word.

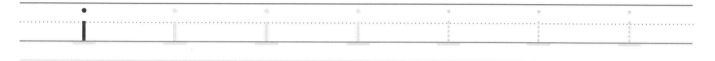

igloo

gloo   gloo

ski

sk   sk

■ Trace the letter. Then write the letter "v" in each word.

vine

vine   ine

glove

glo e   glo e

■ Trace the letter. Then write the letter "w" in each word.

w w w w w w w w

whale

whale   hale

claw

claw   cla

■ Trace the letter. Then write the letter "r" in each word.

r r r r r r r r

road

road   oad

car

car   ca

Lowercase Letters

n, m, x, and z

■ Trace the letter. Then write the letter "n" in each word.

n   n   n   n   n   n   n   n

nut

nut   ut

barn

barn   bar

■ Trace the letter. Then write the letter "m" in each word.

m   m   m   m   m   m   m

mail

mail   ail

clam

clam   cla

■ Trace the letter. Then write the letter "x" in each word.

x   x   x   x   x   x   x

box

bo x   bo ___

fox

fo x   fo ___

■ Trace the letter. Then write the letter "z" in each word.

z   z   z   z   z   z   z

zebra

zebra   ___ebra

fuzzy

fu zz y   fu ___ y

Lowercase Letters Review

i, v, w, r, n, m, x, and z

Name

Date

/ /

To parents/guardians: On this page, your child will review how to neatly write all the lowercase letters taught in this section. If your child can legibly write all the lowercase letters, offer them a lot of praise.

■ Trace the letter. Then write the letter in each word.

ski

sk i   sk   sk

glove

glo v e   glo   e   glo   e

whale

w hale   hale   hale

car

ca r   ca   ca

■ Trace the letter. Then write the letter in each word.

nut

nut   ut   ut

mail

mail   ail   ail

box

box   bo   bo

fuzzy

fuzzy fu y fu y

Lowercase Letters

s, c, o, and e

Name

Date

/ /

■ Trace the letter. Then write the letter "s" in each word.

s   s   s   s   s   s   s

star

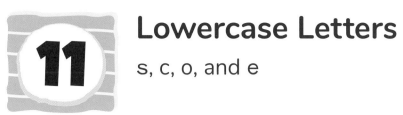

star   tar

grass

grass   gra

■ Trace the letter. Then write the letter "c" in each word.

c   c   c   c   c   c   c

cow

cow   ow

comic

comic   omi

■ Trace the letter. Then write the letter "o" in each word.

o   o   o   o   o   o   o

oval
oval   val

book
book   b k

■ Trace the letter. Then write the letter "e" in each word.

e   e   e   e   e   e   e

egg
egg   gg

bee
bee   b

Lowercase Letters
u and a

■ Trace the letter. Then write the letter "u" in each word.

u   u   u   u   u   u   u

unicorn

unicorn   nicorn

blue

blue   bl e

■ Trace the letter. Then write the letter "a" in each word.

a   a   a   a   a   a   a

apple

apple   pple

tea

tea   te

Lowercase Letters Review

To parents/guardians: On this page, your child will review how to neatly form all the lowercase letters taught in this section. If your child can legibly write all the lowercase letters, offer them a lot of praise.

s, c, o, e, u, and a

■ Trace the letter. Then write the letter in each word.

grass

grass gra___ gra___

cow

cow ___ow ___ow

oval

oval ___val ___val

bee

bee b___ b___

unicorn

unicorn ___nicorn ___nicorn

tea

tea te___ te___

Capital Letters
A to H

To parents/guardians: In this section, your child will practice neatly writing capital letters. Remind your child to always start at the top red line.

■ Trace the letter. Then write the letter in each name.

A A A A A A A A A

Hello, my name is Alex.

Alex   lex

B B B B B B B B

Hello, my name is Brian.

Brian   rian

C C C C C C C

Hello, my name is Claire.

Claire   laire

D D D D D D D D

Hello, my name is Danny.

Danny   anny

■ Trace the letter. Then write the letter in each name.

E E E E E E E E

Hello,
my name is
Eli.

Eli   Eli

F F F F F F F

Hello,
my name is
Fred.

Fred   red

G G G G G G G

Hello,
my name is
Gina.

Gina   ina

H H H H H H H

Hello,
my name is
Harry.

Harry   arry

Capital Letters
I to O

14

Name

Date

/   /

To parents/guardians: Capital letters usually use the entire sentence line. If your child has trouble writing a legible capital letter, remind them that the top of the letter should touch the red line and the bottom should touch the bottom black line.

■ Trace the letter. Then write the letter in each name.

I   I   I   I   I   I   I   I

Hello,
my name is
Isabelle.

sabelle   sabelle

J   J   J   J   J   J   J   J

Hello,
my name is
Jared.

Jared   ared

K   K   K   K   K   K   K   K

Hello,
my name is
Kate.

Kate   ate

L   L   L   L   L   L   L   L

Hello,
my name is
Lauren.

auren   auren

■ Trace the letter. Then write the letter in each name.

M M M M M M M M

Hello, my name is Max.

Max   ax

N N N N N N N N

Hello, my name is Noah.

Noah   oah

O O O O O O O O

Hello, my name is Oliver.

Oliver   liver

Capital Letters
P to V

Name _____

Date ___ / ___ / ___

■ Trace the letter. Then write the letter in each name.

P P P P P P P P P

Hello, my name is Paul.

Paul   aul

Q Q Q Q Q Q Q

Hello, my name is Quinn.

Quinn   uinn

R R R R R R R

Hello, my name is Rachel.

Rachel   achel

S S S S S S S

Hello, my name is Steven.

Steven   teven

■ Trace the letter. Then write the letter in each name.

T T T T T T T T

Hello,
my name is
Theo.

Theo   heo

U U U U U U U U

Hello,
my name is
Ursula.

Ursula   rsula

V V V V V V V V

Hello,
my name is
Vincent.

Vincent   incent

Capital Letters
W to Z

Name   Date
/   /

■ Trace the letter. Then write the letter in each name.

W W W W W W W W

Hello, my name is Will.

Will   ill

X X X X X X X X

Hello, my name is Xavier.

Xavier   avier

Y Y Y Y Y Y Y Y

Hello, my name is Yasmin.

Yasmin   asmin

Z Z Z Z Z Z Z Z

Hello, my name is Zander.

Zander   ander

Capital Letters Review

A to I

To parents/guardians: On this page, your child will review how to neatly form all the capital letters taught in this section. If your child can legibly write all the capital letters, offer them a lot of praise.

■ Trace the letter. Then write the letter in each name.

Alex   lex   lex

Brian   rian   rian

Claire   laire   laire

Danny   anny   anny

Eli   li   li

Fred   red   red

Gina   ina   ina

Harry   arry   arry

Isabelle   sabelle   sabelle

Capital Letters Review

J to Z

■ Trace the letter. Then write the letter in each name.

Jared   ared   ared

Kate   ate   ate

Lauren   auren   auren

Max   ax   ax

Noah   oah   oah

Oliver   liver   liver

Paul   aul   aul

Quinn   uinn   uinn

■ Trace the letter. Then write the letter in each name.

Rachel   achel   achel

Steven   teven   teven

Theo   heo   heo

Ursula   rsula   rsula

Vincent   incent   incent

Will   ill   ill

Xavier   avier   avier

Yasmin   asmin   asmin

Zander   ander   ander

Writing Words

Name

Date

/ /

To parents/guardians: In this section, your child will practice writing word pairs neatly on the sentence lines. This activity will help your child develop the skill of writing words legibly with proper spacing between each word. This is an important skill for building strong handwriting.

■ Trace and write the words on the sentence line. Use the yellow lines (—) and yellow dots (●) for spacing.

red rose

red ● rose

green frog

green ● frog

yellow sun

yellow ● sun

blue kite

blue ● kite

■ Write the words on the sentence line.

What is your favorite flower?

red rose

red rose

What is in the pond?

green frog

What can you see?

yellow sun

What is your favorite toy?

blue kite

Writing Words

Name

Date

/ /

To parents/guardians: The yellow lines and dots on these pages will help your child keep an appropriate space between letters and words. Don't worry too much if your child's letters are a little out of place. Offer your child a lot of praise when they can write each word neatly on the the sentence line.

■ Trace and write the words on the sentence line. Use the yellow lines (—) and yellow dots (●) for spacing.

sunny day

dark cloud

windy night

snow storm

■ Write the words on the sentence line.

What weather is best for the beach?

sunny day

What do you see when it's rainy?

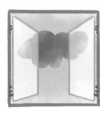

dark cloud

When do you hear leaves blowing?

windy night

When can you make a snowman?

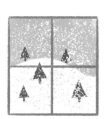

snow storm

Writing Words

Name

Date

/ /

■ Trace and write the words on the sentence line. Use the yellow lines (—) and yellow dots (●) for spacing.

sweet cake

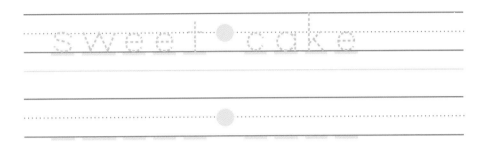

sour apple

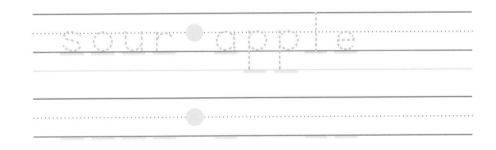

soft bread

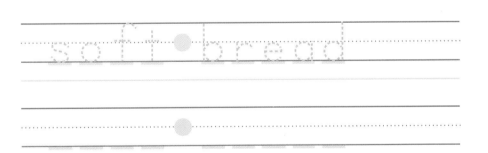

stinky cheese

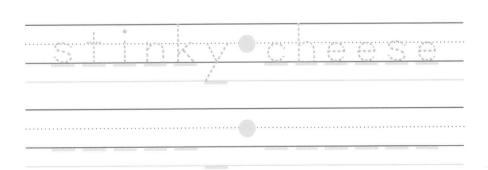

■ Write the words on the sentence line.

What is a delicious treat?

sweet cake

What fruit isn't very sweet?

sour apple

What can you use to make a sandwich?

soft bread

What snack has a strong smell?

stinky cheese

■ Trace and write the words on the sentence line. Use the yellow lines (—) and yellow dots (●) for spacing.

play tennis

swim fast

make lunch

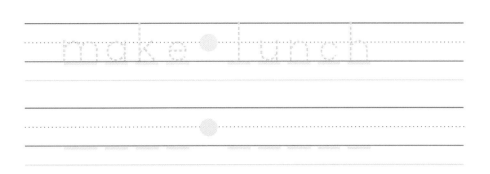

sing loud

■ Write the words on the sentence line.

What is a fun sport to do with a friend?

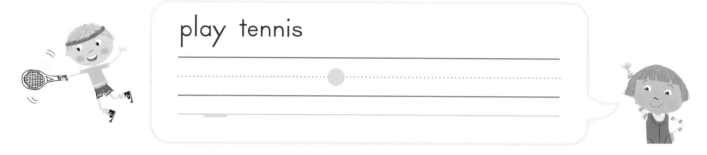

play tennis

What activity can you do in a pool?

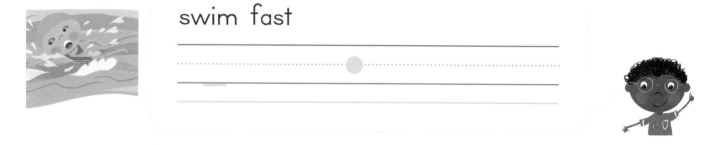

swim fast

What do you do when you're hungry in the middle of the day?

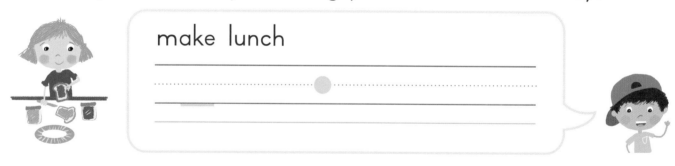

make lunch

What do you do when you hear your favorite song?

sing loud

22 Writing Words

■ Trace and write the words on the sentence line. Use the yellow lines (—) and yellow dots (●) for spacing.

fuzzy chick

fuzzy ● chick

brown cow

brown ● cow

tall horse

tall ● horse

big pig

↓

big ● pig

■ Write the words on the sentence line.

Which animal is small and cute?

fuzzy chick

Which animal makes milk?

brown cow

Which animal runs fast?

tall horse

Which animal has a snout?

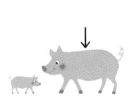

big pig

Writing Words

Name

Date

/   /

■ Trace and write the words on the sentence line. Use the yellow lines (—) and yellow dots (●) for spacing.

one dog

one ● dog

two fish

two ● fish

three birds

three ● birds

four cats

four ● cats

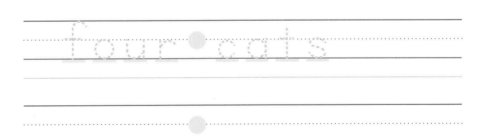

■ Write the words on the sentence line.

How many animals that bark?

one dog

How many animals that swim?

two fish

How many animals that fly?

three birds

How many animals that meow?

four cats

Writing Words

24

■ Trace and write the words on the sentence line. Use the yellow lines (—) and yellow dots (●) for spacing.

square box

round ball

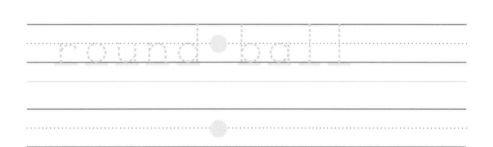

triangle tent

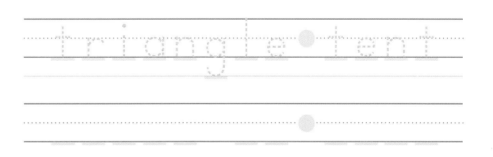

flat paper

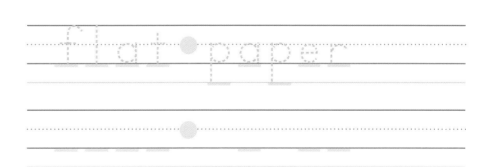

■ Write the words on the sentence line.

What can hold new shoes?

square box

_____

What is fun to play with?

round ball

_____

What do you use when you are camping?

triangle tent

_____

What can you write on?

flat paper

_____

Writing Sentences
with Rhyming Words

Name

Date

/ /

To parents/guardians: In this section, your child will practice writing simple sentences neatly on the sentence lines. This activity will help further develop your child's ability to write words legibly using the proper spacing between each word. When your child finishes each page, you may want to encourage them to read each sentence out loud.

■ Trace the sentence neatly onto the sentence line. Use the yellow dots (●) for spacing.

The cat is fat.

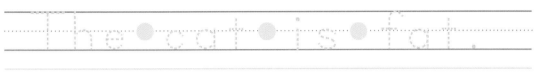

The bed is red.

Two socks in a box.

■ Copy the sentence neatly onto the sentence line.

The cat is fat.

The bed is red.

Two socks in a box.

Writing Sentences
with Rhyming Words

■ Trace the sentence neatly onto the sentence line. Use the yellow dots (●) for spacing.

A pig in a wig.

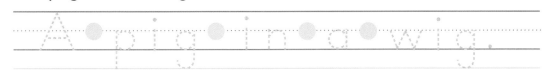

A pup in a cup.

A frog on a log.

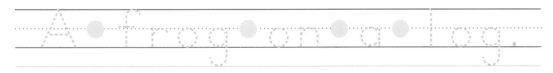

■ Copy the sentence neatly onto the sentence line.

A pig in a wig.

A pup in a cup.

A frog on a log.

Writing Sentences
with Alliterations

■ Trace the sentence neatly onto the sentence line. Use the yellow dots (●) for spacing.

The blue ball bounces.

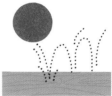

She cooked cookies.

He ran a race.

■ Copy the sentence neatly onto the sentence line.

The blue ball bounces.

She cooked cookies.

He ran a race.

Writing Sentences
with Fun Facts

■ Trace the sentence neatly onto the sentence line. Use the yellow dots ( ) for spacing.

A dog can hear ten times better than a person.

A dog can hear ten

times better than a

person.

Sharks do not have any bones.

Sharks do not have

any bones.

■ Copy the sentence neatly onto the sentence line.

A dog can hear ten times better than a person.

Sharks do not have any bones.

Writing Sentences

with Fun Facts

■ Trace the sentence neatly onto the sentence line. Use the yellow dots (●) for spacing.

There is no sound in outer space.

You can't smell when you are asleep.

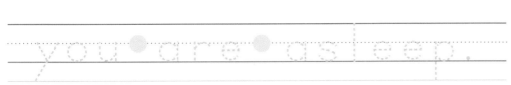

■ Copy the sentence neatly onto the sentence line.

There is no sound in outer space.

You can't smell when you are asleep.

Writing Sentences Review

30

■ Copy the sentence neatly onto the sentence line. Use the yellow dots ( ) for spacing.

The cat is fat.

She cooked cookies.

Two socks in a box.

■ Copy the sentence neatly onto the sentence line.

A frog on a log.

You can't smell when you are asleep.

A dog can hear ten times better than a person.

Writing Activity

Describe the Scene

Name

Date

/ /

To parents/guardians: In this section, your child will describe the scene pictured on the page. Here your child's focus should still be on writing neat and legible sentences rather than spelling the words correctly, which is why the words are provided for the object in each scene. They may also choose to write about objects in the picture that are not labeled. Be sure to praise your child when they have finished writing.

■ Write what you see in this scene.

1. I see a crab.

2. I see a

3. I see a

4. I see a

5. I see a

■ Write what you see in this scene.

swing

bench

sandbox

jump rope

slide

1 I see a slide.

2 I see a

3

4

5

Writing Activity

Describe the Scene

Name

Date

/ /

■ Write what you see in this scene.

1 I see a cow.

2

3

4

5

■ Write what you see in this scene.

tree
bird
sun
car
road

1 I see a car.

2

3

4

5

Writing Activity

Writing Directions

Name

Date

/ /

To parents/guardians: The next two activities ask your child to write directions for a daily task. Have your child look at the images to help them write the steps in the right order.

■ Copy the directions neatly on the sentence line.

How to Get Dressed

1. Pick out clothes.

2. Put on underwear.

3. Put on pants and shirt.

4. Put on socks.

5. Put on shoes.

■ Place the tasks in the correct order and copy below.

How to Get Dressed

○ Put on shoes.

① Pick out clothes.

○ Put on pants and shirt.

○ Put on socks.

○ Put on underwear.

① Pick out clothes.

②

③

④

⑤

Writing Activity
Writing Directions

■ Copy the directions neatly on the sentence line.

How to Wash Your Hands

1. Turn on sink and wet hands.

2. Add soap.

3. Rub hands together.

4. Rinse soap off hands.

5. Dry hands with a clean cloth.

1. Turn on sink and wet hands.

2.

3.

4.

5.

■ Place the tasks in the correct order and copy below.

How to Wash Your Hands

○ Rub hands together.

○ Add soap.

○ Dry hands with a clean cloth.

① Turn on sink and wet hands.

○ Rinse soap off hands.

1 Turn on sink and wet hands.

2 _____

3 _____

4 _____

5 _____

Writing Activity
Writing Cards

To parents/guardians: In this section, your child will practice writing their own words neatly using the skills they have developed earlier in this book. If your child seems to be writing in a hurry, you may want to encourage them to write slowly and carefully. Praise your child when they finish.

■ Use the sample as a guide and write the sentences neatly on the sentence lines.

Dear Sam,
Happy Birthday, Sam!
Have the best day.
From Joe

Dear Sam,

Happy Birthday,

Sam!

Have the best day.

From Joe

■ Use the sample as a guide and write the sentences neatly on the sentence lines.

Dear Sam,
Happy Birthday, Sam!
Have the best day.
From Joe

HAPPY BIRTHDAY

Dear

Writing Activity

Writing Cards

Name

Date

/   /

To parents/guardians: If your child seems to be having difficulty writing their own sentences, you can point to the sample in the upper right corner and say something like, "Look at this carefully and try to write in the same way."

■ Use the sample as a guide and write the sentences neatly on the sentence lines.

Dear Laura,
Happy Birthday,
Laura!
Please eat a lot
of cake.
            From Talia

Happy
Birthday

■ Write your own sentences neatly on the sentence lines. If you have trouble writing your own sentences, you may use the sample.

Dear Laura,
Happy Birthday, Laura!
Please eat a lot of cake.
From Talia

Happy Birthday

Dear

Happy Birthday,

From

Writing Activity

Thank You Notes

37

- Use the sample as a guide and write the sentences neatly on the sentence lines.

Dear Tom,
Thank you for the
birthday gift.
It is fun to play
with.
From Max

THANK YOU

■ Use the sample as a guide and write the sentences neatly on the sentence lines.

THANK YOU

Dear Tom,
Thank you for the
birthday gift.
It is fun to play
with.
        From Max

Writing Activity

Writing a Letter

Name

Date

/ /

To parents/guardians: Writing a letter to a friend is a common activity your child may do to practice their handwriting at school. If your child enjoys the activity in this book, you can have them write a letter to a real friend or family member on a separate piece of paper for extra practice.

■ Use the sample as a guide and write the sentences neatly on the sentence lines.

Hi Tina,

How are you?

How is your family?

What is new with

you recently?

From Lucy

■ Write your own sentences neatly on the sentence lines. If you have trouble writing your own sentences, you may use the sample.

Hello

Hi Tina,
How are you?
How is your family?
What is new with
you recently?
From Lucy

Writing Activity
Free Writing

To parents/guardians: In this last activity, your child will respond to the question in their own words and write sentences neatly on the provided sentence lines. Please check your child's writing to make sure it is legible and that they answered the question using more than one word.

■ Write your response neatly on the sentence lines.

What is your favorite food? Why do you like it?
For example . . .

I like pancakes because they are sweet.
I also like pizza.

■ Write your response neatly on the sentence lines.

What is your favorite place? Why do you like it?

For example . . .

I like the beach because it is hot.
I also like going to the park.

Certificate of Achievement

is hereby congratulated on completing

My Book of Handwriting

Presented on _____, 20____

KUM◯N

Parent or guardian